TABLE OF CONTENTS

INTRODUCTION

The United States has been involved in two major military conflicts in the last

decade. With the conclusion of the War in Iraq in 2011, and U.S. forces set to withdraw

from Afghanistan by the end of 2014, the United States is poised to enter into a new post-

conflict period. An examination of history demonstrates that, for the United States, post-

conflict relates to a shift in the structure and use of other elements of national power.

However, this change is brought on by more than simply the initiation or end of conflict.

These instruments of power also morph to suit the economic environment and adapt to

the world's evolving perceptions of, and attitudes towards, the warring actors. These

three changing dynamics of military strength, economics, and global perception[1] compel

the creation of new or modified sets of diplomatic norms.

The current U.S. financial predicament, driven in great part by the 2008 recession,

presents one of the restrictive circumstances under review. Since the Cold War, the

United States has used a post-conflict "peace dividend"[2] to fund nondefense related

spending. However, the current global and U.S. economic environments make this

practice prohibitive. The United States is not in a position to reinvest Department of

Defense savings into the government's foreign affairs executor, the Department of State.

To complicate matters further, the United States does not enjoy the international

standing it once had. Although not yet defeated or fully discredited, U.S. hegemony is

faltering. Those initial cracks in supremacy put additional pressure on the profession that

---

[1] International standing, global perception, prestige, hegemony, dominion, primacy, prominence, and other descriptive terms are used throughout the document to encapsulate the nebulous third dynamic.

[2] "Peace dividend" refers to an amount of money taken from a defense budget and appropriated to nondefense agencies in times of peace when less money is required for defense than in times of hostility or war.

1

executes the bulk of U.S. foreign policy. The thesis is that an interrelationship exists between U.S. military power, economic strength, its international standing, and the development and use of diplomacy. This interrelationship developed during the late 19th century and continued without need for modification until roughly 2009. The dynamic has changed enough in the last five years to indicate a need to restructure thinking about the interplay between military power, economic power, and the United States' international standing. This new interplay will largely define the upcoming post-conflict period. Therefore, the conduct of U.S. diplomacy must adapt and do so amidst stringent fiscal circumstances and vacillating prestige.

This paper begins by offering some contextual background. Defining diplomacy and foreign policy will show how the relationship between presidents and secretaries of state has affected the prominence of the Department of State in influencing the way the three dynamics relate to each other. The first chapter lays the groundwork for understanding how the diplomatic instrument of national power is used. In so doing, the reader is prepared for the discussion in Chapters 2, 3 and 4 of how certain events created the condition defining U.S. diplomacy in the context of the three-way interplay in place for just over a hundred years. The Spanish-American War, World War I, and World War II are juxtaposed against relevant events in diplomacy in an attempt to explain the interplay between the three dynamics. Although other instances of U.S. involvement in military conflict exist, this paper focuses on just these three for the sake of brevity. Each of these three historical chapters contains a synthesis of how diplomacy has grown to play an increasingly important role in representing U.S. interests and securing international influence. An overview of relevant organizational changes to the

Department of State is included in these syntheses to demonstrate how the interplay affects both the use and structure of the profession of diplomacy.

In Chapter 5 the interrelationship is then observed through the lenses of economic interests and conditions and global leadership. A review of current circumstances will highlight key differences with the past, demonstrating the need for a modified approach to how the United States conducts international affairs. The conclusion offers recommendations intended to adjust the conduct of U.S. diplomacy to the challenges of the 21st century.

CHAPTER 1: DIPLOMACY DEFINED

Contextual Background

The Fine Line between Diplomacy and Foreign Policy

Diplomacy and foreign policy are so closely related that they are often mistakenly used synonymously. Diplomacy and foreign policy are subtly different, just as security and defense are very closely related, yet different. Security could be thought of as the deterrence of a latent threat becoming overt. Defense could be understood as the engagement in conflict resulting in a unilateral victory. Although not strictly analogous, a similar extrapolation is that diplomacy is the tangible conduct of foreign policy. The layman's understanding of this subtle difference is not sufficient for the purpose of this thesis; therefore a brief explanation of the differences is in order.

Diplomacy

U.S. diplomacy is defined as "an instrument of national power, essential for maintaining effective international relationships, and a principal means through which the U.S. defends its interests, responds to crises, and achieves its international goals."[1] Most often it is carried out by career professionals who operate within a distinct set of norms and protocols to officially conduct foreign policy. At times high level strategic players use diplomacy when they directly engage in negotiations and communications, as evidenced when Presidents meet one-on-one or exchange letters. Whether conducted by professional diplomats or by high ranking government officials, diplomacy is the

---

[1] Shawn Dorman, ed., *Inside a U.S. Embassy: Diplomacy at Work*, 3rd ed. (Washington, D.C.: Potomac Books Inc., 2011), 3.

4

execution of a nation's foreign policy. As Thomas Bailey, a noted diplomatic historian observed, "in the military world, grand strategy must be carried out by detailed tactics; in the diplomatic world, fundamental policy must be carried out by implementing policies."[2]

Professional diplomats are versed in world affairs and work to defend national interests by compelling desired actions or ways of thinking from foreign decision makers. A diplomat abroad "talks, listens, reports, analyzes, cajoles, persuades, threatens, debates, and above all negotiates."[3] Chief among a diplomat's duties is the gathering of information that will help strategic decision makers in Washington formulate foreign policies that serve the nation. A diplomat could be thought of as a "kind of licensed spy, he sends home information…[he is] the eyes, ears, and nose of his government."[4] A diplomat "reaches into other societies across barriers of history, culture, language, faith, politics, and economics to build trust, change attitudes, alter behaviors, and keep the peace."[5] Skilled at dissembling and comfortable with ambiguity, U.S. diplomats are the presidentially commissioned and Senate confirmed officers who serve in the profession of diplomacy.

The United States Department of State is the federal executive department charged with engaging in international relations via the practice of diplomacy. Career diplomats conduct both bilateral diplomacy (official interaction between two sovereign nation-states) and multilateral diplomacy (the interaction between multiple nation-states

---

[2] Thomas A. Bailey, *Diplomatic History of the American People* (Englewood Cliffs, N.J.,: Prentice-Hall, 1974) 3.

[3] Harry W. Kopp and Charles A. Gillespie, *Career Diplomacy: Life and Work in the U.S. Foreign Service* (Washington, DC.: Georgetown University Press, 2008), 4.

[4] Bailey, *Diplomatic History of the American People*, 10.

[5] Kopp and Gillespie, *Career Diplomacy: Life and Work in the U.S. Foreign Service*, 4.

and/or international organizations, such as the European Union or the United Nations). The dynamics of multilateral diplomacy are often more complex than bilateral dealings simply because there are more players with distinct agendas.

Although more complex, multilateral negotiation still relies heavily on established, strong bilateral relationships before delving into the more complicated areas. Attempting to build consensus, diplomats start by securing agreement among close allies before identifying potential common ground with other participants. For example, U.S. diplomats would typically form a common understanding with diplomats from any of the "Five Eyes" nations before reaching out to other parties, thereby leveraging collective influence.[6] Multilateral diplomacy is gaining in importance as world matters increasingly involve the linked economic and other interests of several countries.

Foreign Policy

Foreign policy is the expression of national aspirations vis-à-vis interaction with other nations. It comprises national interests such as security, economic prosperity, promulgation of ideology, and an assurance of influence in the global arena. The common belief is that the executive branch of the U.S. government alone creates foreign policy. While it is true that the President crafts and articulates the bulk of foreign policy, the nation's citizens, in actuality, direct the agenda. "The American people themselves, by expressing their attitudes and desires, decide fundamental policies or objectives. The executive branch, by framing specific courses of action, provides implementing policies

---

[6] "Five Eyes" refers to five nations (Australia, Canada, New Zealand, the United Kingdom, and the United States) that constitute the The Technical Cooperation Program. Its aims is to foster cooperation and share resources among the five member nations. Additional information available at: http://www.acq.osd.mil/ttcp/

or tactics."[7] Historically these policies have focused on universal liberty, security, and economic pursuits.

The legislative branch also has a participatory role. For example, the Department of State negotiates treaties that the President signs; however, the authority to approve or deny those treaties rests with the U.S. Senate. Similarly, the executive branch develops foreign aid programs but Congress approves and disburses the funds.

Foreign leaders are becoming acutely aware that the relationships and agreements they develop with executive branch interlocutors are increasingly influenced by the constitutional authority granted to Congress, and by the public's disposition. They therefore have begun to pay closer attention to U.S. domestic politics.

The Department of State is the sole employer of U.S. diplomats. However, it is not the only executor of foreign policy. Five federal agencies make up the Foreign Service: The Department of State, the U.S. Agency for International Development, the Department of Commerce's Foreign Commercial Service, the Department of Agriculture's Foreign Agricultural Service, and the International Broadcasting Bureau. While all five play a role in managing U.S. relationships with the rest of the world, the Department of State is the predominant actor in the conduct of diplomacy and foreign policy.

The President or the Secretary of State: Who Leads Diplomacy?

While it is very clear that ultimately the President sets the nation's foreign policy agenda, increasingly it is the Secretary of State who has played a prominent role in

---

[7] Bailey, *Diplomatic History of the American People*, 3.

leading and shaping diplomacy. "The extent to which the Secretary of State is in the driver's seat usually depends on the temperament of the Chief Executive."[8] The ideal is cooperation between two capable, well-versed and confident leaders, as exemplified by President Harry Truman and Secretary of State George Marshall. This has not always been the case, however.

Past pairings of presidents with particularly strong personalities and weak secretaries of state diminished the advisory role of the Department of State. For example, the domineering combination of President Richard Nixon and National Security Advisor Henry Kissinger ensured that Secretary of State William Rogers remained marginalized. President Nixon "considered Rogers's unfamiliarity with the subject an asset because it guaranteed that policy direction would remain in the White House….Few Secretaries of State can have been selected because of their President's confidence in their ignorance of foreign policy."[9] Nixon and Kissinger collaborated so closely that it was their partnership that allowed Kissinger, while still in his role as National Security Advisor, and before becoming Secretary of State in his own right, to conduct Nixon's notion of détente diplomacy to formalize relations between the United States and China. "They brought out each other's worst qualities, especially paranoia, amorality, an unquenchable desire for praise and recognition, and in Kissinger's case the obsequiousness of the courtier."[10] Had William Rogers been a more formidable Secretary of State, Nixon might not have marginalized the Department of State. Despite their symbiotic relationship, Nixon and Kissinger were not the desirable pairing. "Kissinger might have

---

[8] Bailey, *Diplomatic History of the American People*, 8.

[9] Henry Kissinger, *White House Years* (New York: Simon & Schuster, 2011), 26.

[10] Conrad Black, *Richard M. Nixon: a Life in Full* (New York: Public Affairs, 2007), 843.

done better with a president of greater rectitude, like Truman or Eisenhower (as he did with Gerald Ford). And Nixon might have been better served by a talented but less devious advisor."[11]

Equally unappealing is the grouping of a more passive President and an overly vigorous Secretary of State, as typified by President Dwight Eisenhower and Secretary of State John Foster Dulles according to some historians. Although portrayal of the relationship between Eisenhower and Dulles has sparked much heated debate, "the overwhelming consensus among analysts of United States foreign policy during the Eisenhower administration is that it was dominated by Secretary of State John Foster Dulles. Regardless of their often differing assessment of the policies, these writers agree that Dulles' forceful personality, lengthy preparation, and keen intellect enabled him to control and even manipulate the congenial but bland and passive President Eisenhower.[12] Those that depicted an inverse of this relationship based their information on "appraisals of individuals who were largely outside the inner circles of both the White House and the State Department."[13] Newer material bolsters the opinion that the relationship was disproportional to their professional stations.

Conclusion

Recognizing the subtle difference between diplomacy and foreign policy allows for a clearer understanding of how the interplay between U.S. military engagement, economic strength, and international standing influence the ability of the United States to

---

[11] Black, *Richard M. Nixon: a Life in Full*, 844.

[12] Richard H. Immerman, "Eisenhower and Dulles: Who Made the Decisions?" *Political Psychology* Vol. 1, No. 2 (August 1979), 21.

[13] Ibid.

employ its diplomatic instrument of power. Of equal importance is an understanding of how the relationship between presidents and secretaries of state can affect the prominence of the Department of State. The cadre of career diplomats at the Department of State can offset both the short term nature of secretaryship and an imbalance in the relationship between President and Secretary of State. This group of professionals stabilizes temporary power politics games which might otherwise detrimentally affect relationships the United States has invested years in creating. Fortunately, the ideal delicate balance of interpersonal relationships and expertise has been in place during the last five presidential administrations. It is an important balance that impacts diplomacy's ability to have a hand in steadying the United States' trajectory.

CHAPTER 2: 1890 - 1913 DIPLOMATIC METAMORPHOSIS

Antecedents and the Aftermath

Although diplomacy is often employed to avoid conflict, at times conflict is a direct result of changes in diplomacy and foreign policy. For example, national economic interests may lead to particularly confrontational diplomatic tactics, which in turn, lead to military conflict. U.S. history books generally offer sufficient descriptions of major battles, military strategy, and the men who influenced them. However, very few discuss the diplomacy that shaped those conflicts or how the conduct of diplomacy changed as a result of the outcome of the conflict. Therefore, it is in the side-by-side study of moments when the diplomatic and military instruments converged in history that this paper attempts to explain the interplay between military power, economic power, and international standing. This chapter examines historical events at the turn of the 20th century to demonstrate the interrelationship of these factors that led to a shift in the structure and use of diplomacy.

The Spanish-American War

In 1898, when unable to resolve their differences regarding Cuban independence using diplomacy, and fueled by public anger over the destruction of USS Maine in the Havana harbor, Spain and the United States went to war. Publication of an inflammatory diplomatic communication written by Spanish Ambassador to the United States, Enrique Dupoy de Lôme, which very negatively portrayed the U.S. President, only served to stoke the flames of public outrage.[1] Ancillary to this was the projected French construction of

the Panama Canal. Its obvious importance to U.S. commercial interests presented the

United States with a pretext to intervene and oust Spain from the Caribbean.[2] If able to

secure influence in the Western Hemisphere and gain control of the Panama Canal, the

United States would be poised to not only exponentially speed up the flow of commerce;

it would also be able to more quickly relocate warships, thereby projecting more military

power. In order to secure major routes of transportation and communication, and

therefore have access to the world's markets, the United States would have to have bases

in the Caribbean, the Isthmus, Hawaii, and the Philippines.[3] Its desire for economic

growth meant the United States would have to rely on both military and diplomatic

instruments. "The war was the final act in the struggle for supremacy."[4]

The United States sought supremacy in the Western Hemisphere as a continuation

of the Monroe Doctrine and in order to garner economic growth. "The impingement in

the nineteenth century of what the Supreme Court has called 'the vast external realm'

upon American interests occurred rarely, and usually only when wars between foreign

nations interfered with [U.S.] commerce or when foreign nations intervened in our

---

[1] Tom Lansford, *Theodore Roosevelt in Perspective* (New York: Nova Science Pub Inc, 2005), 44.

[2] J.F.C. Fuller, *The Conduct of War, 1789-1961: a Study of the Impact of the French, Industrial, and Russian Revolutions On War and Its Conduct*, 1st Da Capo Press ed. (New York: Da Capo Press, 1992), 138.

[3] Jerald A. Combs, *American Diplomatic History: Two Centuries of Changing Interpretations* (Berkeley: University of California Press, 1985), 85.

N.B. Combs' book on diplomatic history is unusual in that it is a historiography of U.S. diplomacy and the changing interpretations of events over the years. Combs' methodology complimented my point of view and was therefore a significant source for this thesis.

[4] French Ensor Chadwick, *The Relations Of The United States And Spain: Diplomacy* (Kessinger Publishing, LLC, 2007), 587.

hemisphere."[5] The Spanish-American War was as a result of just such an impingement and marked the beginning of a globally influential United States and its emerging role as an equal amongst the great powers.

The war denoted a turning point in diplomacy as the United States ushered in a new era. "America's resounding victory in the Spanish-American War crystallized the perception of increasing American power both at home and abroad. Having defeated a European great power in battle, America expanded dramatically in the years that followed…having driven Spain out of the Western Hemisphere and with only an accommodating Britain as a European presence in the Americas, the United States chose to fill the resulting vacuum by expanding its influence.[6] The United States employed a new kind of diplomacy to secure that influence.

Anti-imperialists had controlled the direction of U.S. diplomacy in the years preceding the Spanish-American War, thanks in part to a restrained interpretation of the Monroe Doctrine. Politicians were still following President George Washington's advice to avoid the insidious wiles of foreign influence.[7] However, strong domestic public support for going to war ushered in an era of expansionism. This support was a definitive departure from the previously politically popular notion of neutrality and thereby allowed President Theodore Roosevelt to pursue policies that expanded the strategic military and economic interests of the United States.

---

[5] Dean Acheson, *Present at the Creation: My Years in the State Department* (New York: W. W. Norton & Company, 1987), 15.

[6] Fareed Zakaria, *From Wealth to Power: The Unusual Origins of America's World Role* (Princeton: Princeton University Press, 1999), 10.

[7] Combs, *American Diplomatic History: Two Centuries of Changing Interpretations*, 3.

In the aftermath of victory, the United States secured its strategic interests in the Caribbean and the Pacific. "The postwar annexation of the Philippines created a serious and bitter division, but the effort to expel Spain from Cuba was supported by all segments of the population."[8] The Roosevelt Corollary to the Monroe Doctrine put muscle behind U.S. commercial and military goals in the Caribbean. It formally declared the intention to use military force to defend the Western Hemisphere. The United States would intervene in the domestic affairs of states in the Caribbean that could not maintain order or national sovereignty on their own. The United States opposed any intervention in the Western Hemisphere. "To demonstrate America's naval power and counter Japan's growing bellicosity, Roosevelt dispatched the Great White Fleet, sixteen of the navy's most up-to-date battleships."[9]

The Open Door Policy and Dollar Diplomacy

The United States turned to diplomacy between 1899 and 1900 as Secretary of State John Hay constructed what would become known as the Open Door policy. Hay sent diplomatic notes to Japan, Germany, Russia, Britain, France, and Italy, asking them to respect equal trade opportunity for all nations in their spheres.[10] The intent was to advance U.S. trade in the Far East, China in particular. Britain was in favor of Secretary Hay's policy. Britain "had investments in the Philippines, as well as an enormous

---

[8] Combs, *American Diplomatic History: Two Centuries of Changing Interpretations*, 77.

[9] James L. Roark et al., *The American Promise: a History of the United States*, 4th ed. (Boston, MA.: Bedford/St. Martin's, 2009), 668.

[10] Thomas Paterson et al., *American Foreign Relations: a History*, 7th ed. (Boston, MA.: Wadsworth Publishing, 2009), 26.

economic stake in the Far East, and she desired America's support for a policy of equal commercial opportunity."[11]

Between 1909 and 1913, President William Howard Taft implemented Dollar Diplomacy, which aimed to promote U.S. commercial interests and safeguard the nation's economic wellbeing by gaining influence through trade and investment in less developed countries. During his State of the Union address in 1912, President Taft defined this policy by stating:

> The diplomacy of the present administration has sought to respond to modern ideas of commercial intercourse. This policy has been characterized as substituting dollars for bullets. It is one that appeals alike to idealistic humanitarian sentiments, to the dictates of sound policy and strategy, and to legitimate commercial aims. It is an effort frankly directed to the increase of American trade upon the axiomatic principle that the Government of the United States shall extend all proper support to every legitimate and beneficial American enterprise abroad.[12]

President Roosevelt lost an exceptionally capable Secretary of State when John Hay died. From then on President Roosevelt preferred to lead his own diplomatic initiatives, such as resolving the Russo-Japanese War by negotiating the Treaty of Portsmouth. President Taft and Secretary of State Philander Knox were well suited for each other, and therefore, Knox was left to engage in the nation's diplomacy. The ideal power balance between a President and Secretary of State as discussed in Chapter 1 most aptly describes the relationship between Taft and Knox. Together, they crafted a form of diplomacy that allowed the United States to trade freely in Asia and elevated the strategic importance of global influence.

---

[11] Thomas A. Bailey, *Diplomatic History of the American People* (Englewood Cliffs, N.J.,: Prentice-Hall, 1974), 476.

[12] William Howard Taft: "Fourth Annual Message," December 3, 1912. Online by Gerhard Peters and John T. Woolley, The American Presidency Project. http://www.presidency.ucsb.edu/ws/?pid=29553 (accessed February 18, 2012).

During President Taft's tenure, diplomacy's primary goal was to develop the United States as a commercial and financial world power and it did so by protecting the expansion of trade and investment. This was not an entirely new goal. During its earliest years the nation focused on trading with British and Spanish colonies within the Western Hemisphere. Despite prior national interest in foreign trade, Taft's policy was seminal in that it tied economic pursuits to the development of diplomatic and military capabilities. The objective was not only to increase economic opportunities, but also to use non-governmental capital to further national interests. For example, the Department of State "demanded admission of the American bankers into a European banking consortium undertaking construction of the Huguang Railway linking Beijing and Guangzhou.[13]

The United States used its status as an emerging global economic and military power to pursue these new policies that would protect its territories, expand its international commercial and strategic interests, and directly influence international affairs. U.S. success during the Spanish-American War thrust it onto the international stage and created the opportunity for it to pursue commercial interests via use of diplomacy, but also allowed it to make the most of the interplay between military and economic power and prestige.

The State Department Adapts

Growth and Reorganization

Over the course of its history, the Department of State has greatly expanded in size and scope, and this was reflected in to U.S. international prestige. It had only six

---

[13] Paterson et al., *American Foreign Relations: a History*, 56.

employees in 1789 and in less than one hundred years it had increased to 40,000.[14] It is not surprising that the Department of State was minuscule during the 18th century. As a nascent country the United States was otherwise engaged in conquering its own territory and expending within that continent. It was not until after the U.S. Civil War that the United States became a modern industrial unified state on par with Germany, Italy, Britain and France. U.S. diplomacy began to truly emerge and be employed in order to further national economic and strategic interests. Financial capitalism and a demand for new markets abroad captured national focus as the expansion of the territorial frontier ended.[15]

As the nation began to look for external opportunities to advance its strategic interests, the Department of State's role grew in significance, as did its political prominence domestically and internationally. The Department also underwent a reorganization to meet these new international commitments. The State Department is organizationally divided into functional and geographic bureaus. As a reflection of the nation's growing global influence, the bureau system in place was expanded to cover specific geographic regions -- Western Europe, Latin America, the Near East, and the Far East. Additional functional bureaus, such as the Bureau of Trade Relations, were also created.[16]

In addition to expanding the organizational scope, the workforce was also upgraded. New career employees were hired and efforts were also made to improve the professional development of personnel in order to match the stature of foreign diplomats.

---

[14] Bailey, *Diplomatic History of the American People*, 9.

[15] Combs, *American Diplomatic History: Two Centuries of Changing Interpretations*, 186.

[16] United States Department of State Office of the Historian, "A Short History of the Department of State," http://history.state.gov/departmenthistory/short-history (accessed January 23, 2012).

President Taft set up a board of examiners to administer both oral and written examinations to prospective diplomats. He also ordered that vacancies in the higher ranks of secretaries of legations and embassies be filled only from within the career service and that for the purposes of retention and promotion, the efficiency records be maintained for every diplomatic officer and clerk in the Department.[17] As Herbert Peirce once observed, "we would not put a ship into the hands of a commander ignorant of navigation, an army under the control of a general without military training…so we should not put the foreign affairs of our government into the hands of men without knowledge of the various subjects which go to make up the diplomatic science."[18] The Department of State made these improvements in order to elevate the nation's diplomatic standing, making it better prepared to engage at a level of prestige befitting an emerging world power, and taking advantage of the interplay between military and economic power to promoted the United States' international standing.

Conclusion

The U.S. public's strong support for the Spanish-American War allowed the nation to unshackle itself from a neutralist foreign policy. That conflict disrupted the balance of power that had dictated international relations since the beginning of the 19th century. By defeating Spain, the United States emerged as a main world power. It also resulted in Spain ceding possessions -- Puerto Rico, the Philippines, and Guam -- to the United States. As one diplomatic historian observed, "American investments had been the leading cause of the Spanish-American War although these interests had been

---

[17] United States Department of State Office of the Historian, "A Short History of the Department of State," http://history.state.gov/departmenthistory/short-history (accessed January 23, 2012).

[18] Olivia Mae Frederick, Henry P. Fletcher and United States-Latin American Policy, 1910-1930 (Dissertations in American Biography) (Arno Press, 1982), 56.

reinforced by the commercial value of the Philippines and the imperial motivations of men like Theodore Roosevelt."[19] U.S. diplomacy adapted to accommodate this new status and the United States commenced its path to dominance, guided by this new diplomatic bearing. "American diplomacy actively worked to buttress the Monroe Doctrine, with its assertion of American hegemony."[20] Once symbolic, it was now a reality backed by U.S. economic and military power.

The balance in the interrelationship of military and economic might and international standing made it possible for the United States to pursue new diplomatic courses of action, such as the Open Door and Dollar Diplomacy. By the early 20th century, the United States was becoming the world's dominant economic power, thanks to trade and its industrial and agricultural production. "The United States had almost all the attributes of a great power -- it stood ahead or nearly ahead of almost all other countries in terms of population, geographic size and location on two oceans, economic resources, and military potential."[21] The financial stability that it enjoyed enhanced those diplomatic policies and its growing military might.

---

[19] Combs, *American Diplomatic History: Two Centuries of Changing Interpretations*, 185.

[20] Roark et al., *The American Promise: a History of the United States*, 638.

[21] United States Department of State Office of the Historian, "A Short History of the Department of State," http://history.state.gov/departmenthistory/short-history (accessed January 23, 2012).

CHAPTER 3: 1914 - 1936 NEW DIPLOMATIC RELATIONSHIPS

Neutrality and then Intervention

In 1914, true to its traditional suspicion of involvement in European affairs, the United States declared neutrality in the war between the Allied Powers and the Central Powers. Foreign policy issues, such as the Sussex pledge, international trade tariffs, and military interventions in Mexico, were at the forefront of the political debate during the Presidential election campaign of 1916. President Woodrow Wilson's supporters championed his achievements using the slogan "He Kept Us Out of War", and ultimately he won re-election.[1] The concept of dignified restraint kept war fever at bay.

However, neutrality was not a truly viable position for an emerging world power with commercial and private interests extending beyond its borders. Although re-elected on a slogan tacitly promising neutrality, President Wilson's hand was forced once Germany reinitiated unrestricted submarine warfare on U.S. shipping in March of 1917.

Diplomacy played an unsuccessful role in attempting to provide a peaceful solution. "A tense diplomatic conflict with Germany over the legality of unrestricted submarine warfare against neutral shipping simply accelerated a political process that had begun some years earlier."[2] Neutrality quickly became politically untenable. The Department of State struggled to adapt to the instability created by World War I, yet emerged a more respected and modernized agency.

---

[1] Thomas A. Bailey, *Diplomatic History of the American People* (Englewood Cliffs, N.J.,: Prentice-Hall, 1974), 588.

[2] United States Department of State Office of the Historian, "A Short History of the Department of State," http://history.state.gov/departmenthistory/short-history (accessed January 23, 2012).

World War I

Rationale for Intervention

U. S. intervention in World War I has been characterized as necessary to protect U.S. interests, ideology, and even survival against Germany's ruthless autocracy.[3] It is commonly understood that attacks by German submarines violated the United States' neutrality, yet it was more than simply a defense of idealistic neutrality rights that convinced the U.S. politicians and public that intervention was critical. The greater fear was that if Germany was allowed to become a great central empire founded with the prospect that it would dominate Europe, it would severely endanger the safety of the Americas.[4]

An additional and exceptionally rarely discussed rationale for U.S. involvement centers on the financial implications of not siding with the Allies. Wall Street was in favor of the United States intervening in the war to "save the pocketbooks of the bankers and merchants dependent on Allied trade."[5] "These businesses had felt it necessary to save the Allies because their narrow economic interests had become thoroughly tied to those of England and France."[6] U.S. manufacturers and investors had an economic stake in the Allied cause.[7] Yet the argument for this rationale extends beyond the interests of private bankers to that of the public. "The whole citizenry had demanded the prosperity brought by the war trade. Thus, the American people had accepted Allied trade and

---

[3] Jerald A. Combs, *American Diplomatic History: Two Centuries of Changing Interpretations* (Berkeley: University of California Press, 1985), 95.

[4] Ibid.

[5] Ibid, 134.

[6] Ibid, 137.

[7] Bailey, *Diplomatic History of the American People*, 594.

supported loans to the Allies to maintain overseas demand without fully considering how this might entangle America in the war."[8]

The U.S. government's economic entanglement was best explained in a March 5, 1917 diplomatic message from Walter Hines Page, the U.S. Ambassador to Great Britain, in which he warned that unless the United States made a direct government loan to Britain, the Allied war effort would collapse.[9] What contributed to the decision for war was the understanding that "a [U.S.] domestic crisis would flow, in all probability, from the defeat of the Allies or a stalemate that thwarted their ambitions."[10]

However difficult it may be to agree with this interpretation of economic greed and interests having contributed the nation's decision to go to war, it would be naive to not, at a minimum, understand the economic linkages that international trade creates. This war threatened the security of the allied nations, whose economic fates were also clearly embroiled. "In the year before Europe went to war, the U.S. economy had slipped into a recession that wartime disruption of European trade could drastically worsen."[11] Given the established and profitable trade across the Atlantic, the United States' economy was also most certainly intertwined with those of Europe. When President Wilson was asked if the United States would have become involved in the war even if Germany had committed no act of war or injustice against U.S. citizens, Wilson replied, "I think so."[12]

---

[8] Combs, *American Diplomatic History: Two Centuries of Changing Interpretations*, 137.

[9] Ibid.

[10] Charles A. Beard, "The Devil Theory of War", (New York, 1936): pages 18 - 19, quoted in Jerald A. Combs, *American Diplomatic History: Two Centuries of Changing Interpretations* (Berkeley: University of California Press, 1985), 137.

[11] James L. Roark et al., *The American Promise: a History of the United States*, 4th ed. (Boston, MA.: Bedford/St. Martin's, 2009), 689.

[12] Beard, "The Devil Theory of War", pages 98 - 101, quoted in Combs, *American Diplomatic History: Two Centuries of Changing Interpretations*, 138.

Covert Diplomatic Communications Revealed

Germany was becoming not only a threat to the United States' position of neutrality; it was becoming a threat to U.S. status within its hemisphere. The revelation of secret diplomatic communication helped confirm this threat. Documentation under the control of the German Embassy in the United States, which included a German offering of alliance to Mexico in the event the United States entered the war, was intercepted.[13]

This covert attempt at an alliance was found in a diplomatic telegram sent by German Foreign Minister Arthur Zimmerman to the German Ambassador in Mexico City. "The 'Zimmerman Telegram' promised the Mexican Government that Germany would help Mexico recover the territory it had ceded to the United States following the Mexican-American War. In return for this assistance, the Germans asked for Mexican support in the war."[14] In addition to offering an alliance to Mexico, Zimmerman instructed the German Ambassador to extend the alliance to Japan via the Mexican government. The cable read, "as soon as the outbreak of war with the United States of America is certain add the suggestion that [the President of Mexico] should, on his own initiative, invite Japan to immediate adherence and at the same time mediate between Japan and [Germany]."[15]

Although intercepted and decrypted by British naval intelligence on January 19, 1917, the British did not share this bit of intelligence with the United State until after

---

[13] Combs, *American Diplomatic History: Two Centuries of Changing Interpretations*, 95.

[14] United States Department of State Office of the Historian, "Milestones: 1914 - 1920, American Entry into World War I, 1917" http://history.state.gov/milestones/1914-1920/WWI (accessed February 5, 2012).

[15] United States Department of State , "Papers relating to the foreign relations of the United States, 1917. Supplement 1, The World War, Part II: Neutral rights (1917), 147.

Germany resumed its unrestricted submarine warfare in February for fear of the Germans finding out.[16] The British had cracked the German code and did not want that important knowledge revealed. However, the British recognized the criticality of U.S. intervention and decided that swaying U.S. official and public opinion to join the war was worth the risk. The British finally forwarded the intercept to Wilson on February 24th and the American press carried the story the following week.[17] With the threat exposed and encroaching on its backyard, the United States was forced to respond.

Attempts at Peaceful Diplomatic Resolution

President Wilson, a pacifist at heart, was hopeful that the United States could negotiate peace and thereby prevent military involvement. He drafted diplomatic notes appealing to both sets of belligerents, but did not get the intended result. Although the Germans indicated a willingness to discuss terms, the Allies were sorely displeased and mortally offended and were determined not to yield to this "peace threat."[18]

Not only did President Wilson fail to broker the peace negotiation he had hoped to initiate, Germany then escalated the diplomatic dialogue to brinkmanship by proclaiming an unrestricted submarine campaign that would henceforth "attempt to sink all ships -- neutral or belligerent, passenger or merchant -- in the war zone."[19] This was an overwhelming diplomatic setback as it meant the Germans were reneging on the "Sussex pledge."

---

[16] United States Department of State Office of the Historian, "Milestones: 1914 - 1920, American Entry into World War I, 1917" http://history.state.gov/milestones/1914-1920/WWI (accessed February 5, 2012).

[17] Ibid.

[18] Bailey, *Diplomatic History of the American People,* 590.

[19] Ibid.

"Diplomatically, the Sussex was by far the most important ship of the war."[20] Wilson had threatened to sever diplomatic relations with Germany following the sinking of the Sussex unless Germany refrained from attacking all passenger ships and allowing the crews of enemy merchant vessels to escape from their ships prior to any attack.[21] The Germans had accepted those terms on May 4, 1916. By declaring that diplomatic relations would be severed if the Germans broke this pledge, which meant that the United States would most probably be drawn into the war, Woodrow Wilson's hands were tied as soon as the Germans made their proclamation.[22] "He dramatically appeared before Congress, on February 3, 1917, to announce the termination of diplomatic intercourse with Germany."[23]

Not only were U.S. lives being lost as a result of the Germans waging war on U.S. shipping, but the U.S. economy was also suffering. In the face of such threat, unarmed commercial vessels chose instead to halt foreign trade. "Great quantities of wheat and cotton were piling up on the wharves, and threatening to dislocate American economic life."[24] Hoping to prevent further economic and human loss, President Wilson found legal authority that allowed him to mount guns on U.S. vessels for self defense. Although helpful, severing diplomatic relations and arming commercial vessels was not enough to ensure U.S. national interests were protected. "America could not afford to

---

[20] Bailey, *Diplomatic History of the American People,* 590, 584.

[21] United States Department of State Office of the Historian, "Milestones: 1914 - 1920, American Entry into World War I, 1917" http://history.state.gov/milestones/1914-1920/WWI (accessed March 7, 2012).

[22] Bailey, *Diplomatic History of the American People*, 585.

[23] Ibid.

[24] Ibid, 592.

rely on protests designed to await settlement at the end of the war."[25] The United States would have to finally intervene in the war it had spent years avoiding. As captured by the following commentary in a Philadelphia newspaper, the "difference between war and what we have now is that now we aren't fighting back."[26]

The United States Goes to War

Once the United States was fully aware of the threat that Germany posed, and with diplomatic resolution thwarted, military involvement was inevitable. As a maturing global power, the United States had too much at stake in this battle for worldwide influence. Reverting to a true form of isolationism was unthinkable. "The Zimmermann telegram and the destruction of American trade persuaded even the most pacifistic areas of the United States of the necessity for war."[27] On April 2, 1917, President Woodrow Wilson went before a joint session of Congress to request a declaration of war against Germany. "Wilson cited Germany's violation of its pledge to suspend unrestricted submarine warfare in the North Atlantic and the Mediterranean, and its attempts to entice Mexico into an alliance against the United States, as his reasons for declaring war."[28] Wilson's memorable war message asked Congress to accept the status of belligerency

---

[25] Charles Seymour, "American Neutrality, 1914 - 1917," (New Haven and London, 1935): pages 9 - 10, quoted in Jerald A. Combs, *American Diplomatic History: Two Centuries of Changing Interpretations* (Berkeley: University of California Press, 1985), 147.

[26] Bailey, *Diplomatic History of the American People*, 593.

[27] Seymour, "American Diplomacy During the World War," page 203, quoted in Combs, *American Diplomatic History: Two Centuries of Changing Interpretations*, 148.

[28] United States Department of State Office of the Historian, "Milestones: 1914 - 1920, American Entry into World War I, 1917" http://history.state.gov/milestones/1914-1920/WWI (accessed February 5, 2012).

that had been "thrust" upon the United States. By this time the U.S. people were resigned to fighting.[29]

The State Department Adapts

Carving Out a New Role

The fundamental shift in foreign policy that accompanied World War I posed great challenges for the Department of State as it assumed duties never anticipated in earlier years.[30] The Department was forced to take on responsibilities it was ill equipped to handle. In recognition, Congress authorized a significant number of new permanent positions, including 27 in the Diplomatic Service, for a total of 97. The domestic complement grew from 234 employees in 1910 to 708 one decade later. Expenditures jumped from $4.9 million in 1910 to $13.6 million in 1920.[31]

This increase in prominence was tied to an increase in foreign affairs. The U.S. public had held a general sense of apathy for the practice of diplomacy and the matter of foreign policy during the era of isolationism. This favorable attention gave rise to the term "new diplomacy," which described a statecraft responsive to the desires of popular majorities, which brought international politics and its practitioners fully into the consciousness of people who had never before been concerned with foreign relations.[32]

---

[29] Bailey, *Diplomatic History of the American People*, 593.

[30] United States Department of State Office of the Historian, "A Short History of the Department of State," http://history.state.gov/departmenthistory/short-history (accessed January 23, 2012).

[31] Ibid.

[32] United States Department of State Office of the Historian, "A Short History of the Department of State," http://history.state.gov/departmenthistory/short-history (accessed February 5, 2012).

Not only did diplomacy grow in importance in public opinion, so did it among the profession of educated historical authors. "The post-World War I era also saw the emergence of diplomatic history as a separate and identifiable discipline within the historical profession." [33] Although no match for the volumes upon volumes written about military strategy and conflict, a study of historiography reveals that this period was a turning point for U.S. diplomacy.

Who is Leading Diplomacy Now?

Precisely at the time when the Department of State was gaining in standing and diplomacy was becoming relevant to the common citizen, the Department's influence was not big enough for its britches. "Almost all the significant decisions of the conflict -- to pursue strict neutrality in 1914, to intervene on behalf of the Allies in 1917, to champion the League of Nations in 1918, and to negotiate a peace treaty on American terms in 1919 -- emanated from the White House without decisive contributions from the Secretary of State and his subordinates."[34] As described in Chapter 1, the parings of President Wilson and the two Secretaries of State during World War I -- William Jennings Bryan and Robert Lansing, were not ideal. President Wilson did not have a close and confidential relationship with either of them and instead he relied primarily on the advice of intimate friends like Edward M. House of Texas.[35]

---

[33] Combs, *American Diplomatic History: Two Centuries of Changing Interpretations*, 115.

[34] United States Department of State Office of the Historian, "A Short History of the Department of State," http://history.state.gov/departmenthistory/short-history (accessed March 7, 2012).

[35] United States Department of State Office of the Historian, "A Short History of the Department of State," http://history.state.gov/departmenthistory/short-history (accessed March 7, 2012).

In addition to not serving as the principal source of advice, "a less obvious but equally significant factor was that the Department was poorly organized to meet the requirements of wartime. It tended to act slowly, and it lacked expertise in dealing with military issues."[36] The Department of State might have understood political ends, but it was unfamiliar with military means, and so it lacked "the expertise and institutions [needed] to exert dominant influence on the shaping of grand strategy.[37]

Lastly, the Department was not prepared for the interagency effort required of such national emergencies. The required participation of the War Department, the Navy Department, and the Treasury, among others, was new and the Department of State was not prepared to take a leading role in coordinating these activities.[38]

Modernization of the Department

Although the Department of State underwent major changes in how officers were appointed to certain positions and administratively reassigned, the public believed the modernization was far from complete. [39] "In January 1920, Secretary of State Robert Lansing, writing to a sympathetic Congressman, John Jacob Rogers of Massachusetts, described the problem: "The machinery of government provided for dealing with our foreign relations is in need of complete repair and reorganization. As adequate as it may have been when the old order prevailed and the affairs of the world were free from the present perplexities it has ceased to be responsive to present needs."

---

[36] Ibid.

[37] Harry W. Kopp and Charles A. Gillespie, *Career Diplomacy: Life and Work in the U.S. Foreign Service* (Washington, DC.: Georgetown University Press, 2008), 15.

[38] United States Department of State Office of the Historian, "A Short History of the Department of State," http://history.state.gov/departmenthistory/short-history (accessed March 7, 2012).

[39] Ibid.

The Department of State set about enacting the following three necessary reforms in order to appropriately adjust to post-conflict conditions:

(I) The foreign services had to be fully professionalized and democratized;

(II) The structure of the Department had to be modernized to deal effectively with a whole range of new policy initiatives; and

(III) Relations between the Department and other participants in the foreign policy process had to be clarified and conducted in a new institutional context.[40]

The Nation Reverts

Despite the reforms, the Department of State did not modernize enough to completely distance itself from past tendencies. The lack of progress "reflected the country's lack of commitment to an energetic foreign policy."[41] The nation was not fully ready to accept the responsibilities commensurate with the power bestowed on a global leader, as envisioned by President Wilson, and as a result, the Department of State returned to the passivity of the 19th century, and accepted a secondary role.[42] By the time Secretary of State Cordell Hull assumed control of the Department in 1933, he found an agency that was "small, placid, comfortably adjusted to the lethargic diplomacy of the preceding decade, and suffused with habits of thought that reached back to a still earlier day." [43] Lasting change would not occur until after World War II.

---

[40] United States Department of State Office of the Historian, "A Short History of the Department of State," http://history.state.gov/departmenthistory/short-history (accessed March 14, 2012).

[41] Ibid.

[42] Ibid.

[43] United States Department of State Office of the Historian, "A Short History of the Department of State," http://history.state.gov/departmenthistory/short-history (accessed March 14, 2012).

Conclusion

The end of this period saw the United States become an active player on the international scene. It engaged in action both in its traditional 'sphere of influence' in the Western Hemisphere and in Europe during the First World War.[44] Despite a strong desire for neutrality during World War I, it was impracticable. Although permanent change would take a few more years to cement, once the United States took the position of involvement, the United States was "not likely to remain neutral again in any war which involved the balance of power in the world of destinies of the major portion of mankind."[45] "Woodrow Wilson was at the height of his prestige on the eve of the Paris Peace Conference. He had led a united America into World War I and invested intervention with a moral purpose."[46]

---

[44] United States Department of State Office of the Historian, "Milestones: 1914 - 1920, American Entry into World War I, 1917" http://history.state.gov/milestones/1914-1920/WWI (accessed February 5, 2012).

[45] John Holladay Latané, "From Isolation to Leadership: A Review of American Foreign Policy", (New York, 1918): pages 179 - 186, quoted in Jerald A. Combs, *American Diplomatic History: Two Centuries of Changing Interpretations* (Berkeley: University of California Press, 1985), 96.

[46] Combs, *American Diplomatic History: Two Centuries of Changing Interpretations*, 117.

CHAPTER 4: 1936 - 1945 DIPLOMATIC CHALLENGES

Precursors to World War II

World War II is considered by most to be a continuation of World War I due to the inadequacies of the Treaty of Versailles. The Paris Peace Conference established a new world order that was to be maintained by means embodied in the League of Nations. However, it was not universally accepted. Not only were many of the major powers -- notably the United States and Soviet Russia -- outside of the League, but also a number of states were ideologically opposed to the entire underpinnings of the new system.[1]

Two things contributed significantly to altering the status quo during the interwar years. Firstly, Japan withdrew from the League in 1936 after its assault on Manchuria drew condemnation from the collective. Secondly, World War I victors, the Allied nations, insisted on large reparation payments from Germany, which created a web of debts and sapped Europe's economic vitality.[2] Severe inflation and recession in Germany led to political disenchantment, which gave rise to Adolf Hitler and the Nazi Party. This rise was advanced by global financial and economic instability caused by the Wall Street crash of late 1929.[3]

---

[1] Andrew Dorman and Greg Kennedy, eds., *War and Diplomacy: from World War I to the War On Terrorism* (Washington, D.C.: Potomac Books Inc., 2008), 27.

[2] James L. Roark et al., *The American Promise: a History of the United States*, 4th ed. (Boston, MA.: Bedford/St. Martin's, 2009), 742.

[3] Ibid, 28.

Wartime industry during World War II not only pulled the U.S. economy out of depression, it generated great profits that resulted in the United States emerging as one of the foremost economic, political, and military powers in the world. [4] "The gross national product soared to four times what it had been when Roosevelt became president in 1933."[5] As Europe and Asia struggled to rebuild their shattered post-war economies, the United States enjoyed the strongest economy in the world. "As the dominant Western nation in the postwar world, the United States asserted its leadership in the reconstruction of Europe while occupying Japan and overseeing its economic and political recovery."[6] The United States implemented the concept of foreign aid as a tool of diplomacy. Economic assistance became a strategic element of foreign policy and offered significant assistance to worn-torn countries in Europe and Asia.

European Recovery Program

During a speech given to the graduating class at Harvard University in 1947, Secretary of State George Marshall gave shape to the concept of foreign aid when he issued a call for an assistance program to rebuild Europe. Under Secretary of State Dean Acheson argued that providing aid to rebuild Western Europe was a matter of U.S.

---

[4] United States Department of State Office of the Historian, "Milestones: 1945-1952, The Early Cold War" http://history.state.gov/milestones/1945-1952 (accessed February 5, 2012).

[5] Roark et al., *The American Promise: a History of the United States*, 824.

[6] Ibid, 825.

national self-interest.[7] He delivered a speech -- what President Truman called the prologue to the Marshall Plan -- in which he articulated the national interest as follows:

> Not only do human beings and nations exist in narrow economic margins, but also human dignity, human freedom, and democratic institutions. It is one of the principal aims of our foreign policy today to use our economic and financial resources to widen these margins. It is necessary if we are to preserve our own freedoms and our own democratic institutions. It is necessary for our national security.[8]

Europe had been ravaged by World War II and was susceptible to a threat of Communist revolution. Congress, fearing Communist expansion and the potential deterioration of linked U.S. - European economies, passed the Economic Cooperation Act in March 1948 and approved funding that would eventually rise to more than $12 billion for the rebuilding of Western Europe.[9] The Marshall Plan stimulated an already growing U.S. economy by generating a resurgence of European industrialization, which attracted extensive investment, and established markets for U.S. goods.

A New Approach to National Security

The National Security Act of 1947 had a weighty effect on the nation's approach to security. Not only did it unite the different military branches under a single Secretary of Defense, it also profoundly affected the Department of State. The National Security Council was created to coordinate defense, foreign, and domestic policy under the chairmanship of the President. Legislature dictated that it be comprised of only six

---

[7] Roark et al., *The American Promise: a History of the United States*, 835.

[8] Dean Acheson, *Present at the Creation: My Years in the State Department* (New York: W. W. Norton & Company, 1987), 229.

[9] United States Department of State Office of the Historian, "Milestones: 1945-1952, The Early Cold War" http://history.state.gov/milestones/1945-1952/MarshallPlan (accessed February 5, 2012).

permanent members: the Secretaries of State, Defense, Army, Navy, and Air Force, and the Chairman of the National Resources Board. The President could designate the heads of other executive departments, such as the Director of the new Central Intelligence Agency, to attend if needed.[10]

The creation of the NSC meant new responsibilities for the Department of State. The Secretary of State was named as the ranking member in the President's absence, and the Department of State controlled the NSC and its operations. The State Department's Policy Planning Staff wrote most of the NSC's papers, which after discussion by the Council and approval by Truman, were then disseminated to the bureaucracy in summary form as NSC actions.[11]

It is important to note that the NSC did not displace the Secretary of State as the President's senior adviser on international questions; it simply required all agencies to contribute to the decision-making process. The NSC was intended to correct the failures of interagency coordination between 1914 and 1945. It became the mechanism through which the Department of State could exert consistent influence on national security policy. But the Department of State could only realize its full potential in the new institutional context if the Secretary of State gained the confidence of the President.[12] The relationship between the President and the Secretary of State is critical to careful formulation of U.S. foreign policy and the conduct of diplomacy, which ultimately have a hand in shaping the country's international prestige.

---

[10] United States Department of State Office of the Historian, "A Short History of the Department of State," http://history.state.gov/departmenthistory/short-history (accessed March 3, 2012).

[11] Ibid.

[12] Ibid.

The State Department Adapts

As had occurred previously, the end of the war brought organizational changes.
The introduction of foreign aid as a tool of diplomacy was evolutionary and meant that
the Department would have to elevate economics to be on par with other strategic issues.
The Department created a new Under Secretary for Economic Affairs in August 1946 to
manage the complex economic component of U.S. foreign policy. The Under Secretary
supervised international economic activities and established effective relations with the
International Bank for Reconstruction and Development (IBRD), the International
Monetary Fund (IMF), and the UN's Food and Agriculture Organization (FAO).[13]

As the Secretary of State's level of influence and responsibilities grew after
World War II, so did the required qualifications of potential incumbents. Candidates for
the office of Secretary of State were chosen because they possessed broad foreign policy
experience and the management skills deemed essential to effective performance.
Secretaries traveled extensively to negotiate and coordinate with their foreign
counterparts and chiefs of state. Although the burdens of office increased exponentially,
Secretaries also gained prestige, as a consequence of the high priority now accorded to
foreign relations.[14]

---

[13] United States Department of State Office of the Historian, "A Short History of the Department of State," http://history.state.gov/departmenthistory/short-history (accessed January 23, 2012).

[14] Ibid.

Conclusion

The Department of State emerged from World War II better prepared to lead the foreign policy process.[15] The expansion of the United States' international power, responsibilities, and presence after World War II presented challenges and opportunities.[16] The Marshall Plan institutionalized and legitimized the concept of U.S. foreign aid programs, which became an integral part of U.S. foreign policy.[17] Whereas President Taft's dollar diplomacy used private capital to leverage and further U.S. interests, President Truman used public capital.[18] Historians have limned how Taft's policies from the early 1900s in support of the expansion of U.S. business have been adapted and carried through to 21st century initiatives, such as President Clinton's North American Free Trade Agreement, or the decision to engage China on economic issues.[19]

At the end of World War II, U.S. military, economic, and technological power was unquestionable. The United States had a monetary monopoly on nuclear weapons; the largest navy; a massive long-range strategic air force; commanded more than half the planet's manufacturing capacity; held most of the world's gold stocks and foreign currency reserves; was the leading petroleum producer; and possessed the only intact large-scale advanced industrial economy on the globe, robustly invigorated by the war.[20]

---

[15] United States Department of State Office of the Historian, "A Short History of the Department of State," http://history.state.gov/departmenthistory/short-history (accessed March 3, 2012).

[16] Harry W. Kopp and Charles A. Gillespie, *Career Diplomacy: Life and Work in the U.S. Foreign Service* (Washington, DC.: Georgetown University Press, 2008), 18.

[17] United States Department of State Office of the Historian, "Milestones: 1945-1952, The Early Cold War" http://history.state.gov/milestones/1945-1952/MarshallPlan (accessed February 5, 2012).

[18] Encyclopedia of the American Foreign Relations, "New American Nation: Dollar Diplomacy," http://www.americanforeignrelations.com/A-D/Dollar-Diplomacy.html (accessed March 16, 2012).

[19] Ibid.

[20] Andrew J. Bacevich, ed., *The Short American Century: a Postmortem* (Cambridge, Mass.: Harvard University Press, 2012), 32.

U.S. leaders leveraged this incontestable power to transform global politics and the United States' role in it. "The United States exercised the power that World War II bestowed upon it to affect a revolution in international affairs."[21]

---

[21] Bacevich, ed., *The Short American Century: a Postmortem*, 16.

CHAPTER 5: CONVERGENCE OF ECONOMIC INFLUENCE AND HEGEMONY

U.S. Dominion

The preceding chapters outlined how U.S. economic interests have historically had a hand in driving the creation of new foreign policy, which in turn has driven the creation of new diplomacy. Those diplomatic methods and tactics were successful in great part because they were supported by the threat of, or actual employment of, military might. The synergistic interplay of these three elements of national power, and their strategic use throughout the 20th century provided the United States with a peerless level of dominion over the world. The United States grew into its sole superpower status thanks to a balance in that interrelationship. In order to understand what aspects of this interplay have changed, this chapter will explore the lead up to current economic conditions, and will show how they relate to U.S. hegemony.

A Legacy of Control and Influence

The United States uses several different economic measures to induce political and commercial behavior of other nations. Military doctrine teaches that the purpose of one of the principles of war, mass, "is to concentrate the effects of combat power at the place and time to achieve decisive results."[1] And so it follows that economic measures intended to alter how another country conducts its affairs must be marshaled. These

---

[1] U.S. Joint Staff, *Joint Publication 1, Joint Warfare of the Armed Forces of the United States* (Washington DC: Joint Chiefs of Staff, 14 November 2000), B-1

efforts can be positive incentives, as is the case with foreign aid and extensions of credit. They may also be punitive actions, such as restricting trade or applying high tariffs. The United States developed such economic measures as a result of its increased economic might after World War II. "In 1939 the U.S. economy had been about one-half the size of the combined economies of Europe, Japan, and the Soviet Union. Ten years later, it was larger than those combined economies."[2]

As a result of the United States' economic and military strength, the U.S. government asserted a new determination to shape international affairs in the post-World War II world. John Ikenberry, a distinguished international relations theorist, catalogued the following list of institutions created after World War II that transmogrified how dominant world powers such as the United States interacted and leveraged influence:

> The UN, with its headquarters welcomed on the soil of America's principal city; the International Monetary Fund (IMF), designed to stabilize international exchange rates and encourage fiscal discipline; the International Bank for Reconstruction and Development, better known as the World Bank, to finance postwar reconstruction and foster worldwide economic growth; and the General Agreement on Tariffs and Trade, which would later evolve into the World Trade Organization (WTO), to reduce tariff barriers and liberalize world commerce.[3]

"For nearly three generations those institutions sustained a remarkable passage in the world's history. They constituted the major pillars underlying an international economic expansion of unprecedented reach."[4]

---

[2] Frederick S. Weaver, *The United States and the Global Economy: from Bretton Woods to the Current Crisis* (Lanham: Rowman & Littlefield Publishers, 2011), 16.

[3] Andrew J. Bacevich, ed., *The Short American Century: a Postmortem* (Cambridge, Mass.: Harvard University Press, 2012), 33.

[4] Ibid, 35.

1944: A Framework for the International Economy

U.S. economic dominion began when an Allied victory became imminent. Representatives from 44 nations convened in 1944 at an international conference in Bretton Woods, New Hampshire to design a new framework that codified an international monetary system for capitalist economies.[5] Two of the institutions listed by Ikenberry, the IMF and the World Bank, were created as a result of the conference and are still sources of significant economic leverage today.

These two institutions operate in concert as both work with nations experiencing international deficits. "The IMF's primary responsibility [is] to deal with imbalances considered to be of a short-term, cyclical nature. It [does] this by allowing a deficit nation to withdraw in hard currency (for example, U.S. dollars) the equivalent of its IMF quota."[6] The World Bank is responsible for providing financial assistance for the reconstruction of war-ravaged nations and the economic development of less developed countries.[7] World Bank loans are long-term and are meant to bring about economic reform that would help improve competitiveness. Influence and power in both organizations is proportional to the quota each nation pays into the institutions, and therefore the United States has had little trouble dominating both institutions. In fact, the United States wielded so much economic power after World War II that the Marshall

---

[5] Frederick S. Weaver, *The United States and the Global Economy: from Bretton Woods to the Current Crisis,* 16.

[6] Ibid, 22.

[7] United States Department of State Office of the Historian, "Milestones: 1937-1945: The Bretton Woods Conference, 1944" http://history.state.gov/milestones/1937-1945/BrettonWoods (accessed April 6, 2012).

Plan eclipsed both World Bank and IMF financing during reconstruction of Western Europe.[8]

Current Conditions

There is a striking difference between previous periods of post-conflict economic conditions when the nation enjoyed budget surpluses and economic stability and those of current day. Interestingly, there is a commonality to both of the global economic crises of the past 100 years -- a precipitous drop in the U.S. economy. "The U.S. stock market crash of 1929, an economic downturn in Germany, and financial difficulties in France and Great Britain all coincided to cause a global financial crisis."[9] Similarly, the 2008 U.S. recession has played a role in the European financial crises and current global recession. The economic downturn in the United States contributed to the global economic and financial crisis thanks to two factors: First, foreign financial institutions bought a lot of the mortgage-backed securities issued in the United States and then experienced losses just like those on Wall Street, and second, the U.S. economic crisis triggered a severe drop in world trade.[10]

Even as a hegemon, the current global and domestic economic environments make unilateral action prohibitive for the United States. "President Obama inherited a United States that was in a state of financial crisis that was deeply rooted in the nation's

---

[8] Frederick S. Weaver, *The United States and the Global Economy: from Bretton Woods to the Current Crisis* (Lanham: Rowman & Littlefield Publishers, 2011), 24.

[9] United States Department of State Office of the Historian, "Milestones: 1921-1936, The Great Depression and U.S. Foreign Policy" http://history.state.gov/milestones/1921-1936/GreatDepression (accessed February 5, 2012).

[10] Martin Neil Baily and Douglas J. Elliott, *The US Financial and Economic Crisis:Where Does It Stand and Where Do We Go From Here?* (Washington D.C.: Brookings, 2009), 16.

failing private financial institutions, which by early 2009 acted to undermine both the global and U.S. economies."[11]

In addition to unilateral action being economically prohibitive, it is increasingly detrimental to the United States' international standing. The world has grown weary and is less amenable to projection of U.S. economic and military power.

Shrinking Defense Capabilities

As we enter into a new post-conflict period of economic austerity, the U.S. government will grapple with determining the appropriate levels of defense funding commensurate with national security risks. "The wars in Iraq and Afghanistan that defined the last decade are winding down as persistent and new threats compete for our attention. Meanwhile, budgetary pressure has already forced cuts to defense spending, and additional automatic reductions, known as the sequester, will go into effect in 2013."[12]

The use of military power will become politically more complex and operationally more difficult as funding dwindles. "The United States will remain the single most powerful country but will be less dominant. Shrinking economic and military capabilities may force the U.S. into a difficult set of tradeoffs between domestic versus foreign policy priorities."[13]

---

[11] Allan Watson. "U.S. Hegemony and the Obama Administration: Towards a New World Order?" Antipode 42, 2 (2010), 242.

[12] Bipartisan Policy Center's Economic Policy Program and National Security Program, *Indefensible: The Sequester's Mechanics and Adverse Effects on National and Economic Security* (Washington D.C., 2012), 4.

[13] Office of the Director of National Intelligence (U.S.), ed., *Global Trends 2025: A Transformed World*, 4, (Washington, DC: Central Intelligence Agency, 2008), iv.

"Our nation faces a serious fiscal challenge, which requires making difficult budgetary decisions. Without action, growing deficits and debt will erode our prosperity and leadership role in the world."[14]

Globalization and Future Trends

The world is in transition. Global Trends 2025, a behemoth report produced by the National Intelligence Council, depicts some of the critical medium term global risks and challenges as emanating from increased global urbanization. An imminent youth bulge in underdeveloped countries, coupled with emerging economic growth of developing nations, means food and water supplies will be in even greater demand in the next 15 years. Climate change, which is inevitable, and the adoption by a growing middle class of a typical Western diet which is resource inefficient, will further exacerbate the problem. This will lead to economic disruption, political instability, population stresses, civil unrest, and conflict. Where these conditions converge is considered an "arc of instability."[15] Disenfranchised people living along that arc are becoming more susceptible to non-state actors as they gain influence.

Diplomacy will be an increasingly decisive source of competitive advantage. U.S. diplomacy needs to be able to shape this difficult global operating environment in favorable ways.

---

[14] Bipartisan Policy Center's Economic Policy Program and National Security Program, *Indefensible: The Sequester's Mechanics and Adverse Effects on National and Economic Security* (Washington D.C., 2012), 5.

[15] As decribed in the *Global Trends 2025* report, countries with youthful age structures and rapidly growing populations mark a crescent or "arc of instability" stretching from the Andean region of Latin America across Sub-Saharan Africa, the Middle East and the Caucasus, and through the northern parts of South Asia.

Diplomatic battles of the future will be global and economic in nature. Some say that the United States in the future won't have the dominance it has enjoyed relative to the rest of the world, so that economic negotiations will be more difficult and more important. And if you're out there promoting democracy and the rule of law, you've got to be able to articulate the economic advantages, you've got to be able to answer the question, "What's in it for me?" You need to understand the linkages in a society -- between regions, tribes, political parties -- where the underlying economics are more important than the political overlay.[16]

Faltering Hegemony

What Provokes Global Antipathy

An outpouring of sympathy in the aftermath of the September 11, 2001 terrorist attacks on the United States hushed the grumblings of those displeased with U.S. hegemony. However, the militant rhetoric of U.S. politicians and leaders, and a willingness to use force without international legitimacy since have allowed anti-Americanism to spread and grow in strength. "The fact that America possesses peerless global political clout makes it the focus of envy, resentment, and for some, intense hatred."[17] The fact that the United States is unrivaled in so many ways makes it foreordained that it will be the target of antagonism, yet there is still much that can be done to lessen this, and should be done because it diminishes the United States' prestige. It is important to understand what factors provoke global antipathy because it weakens U.S. influence.

---

[16] Marianne Myles, interview Augutst 2007, quoted in Harry W. Kopp and Charles A. Gillespie, *Career Diplomacy: Life and Work in the U.S. Foreign Service* (Washington, DC.: Georgetown University Press, 2008), 189.

[17] Zbigniew Brzezinski, *The Choice: Global Domination or Global Leadership* (New York: Basic Books, 2004), viii.

Economic Disparity

Many in the international community point to the vast economic disparity as their principal reason for frustration with the United States. However, it is more than simply the fact that the United States is a nation of great wealth, it is about how it uses that wealth and power. Foreigners believe the heavy-handed practice of trading economic aid for political reform to be an unjust cloaked form of duplicitous economic warfare that only further exacerbates the economic disparity between wealthy nations, and those in need of economic aid. Economic warfare, in its true sense, is used during conflict against a warring actor to "cut the enemy's supplies, information, and funds from foreign territory and prevent his communication with it."[18] Since the United States is not at war or engaged in military conflict with these nations, what the disgruntled foreigners are actually referring to is the influence the United States has over international organizations such as the IMF and World Bank. The hostility comes from not only the economic leverage that the United States wields, but also from the control it has over the institutions they feel shackle their nations economic survival to U.S. political machinations.

Hubris and Aggrandizing Projection of Power

Hermann Eduard Von Holst, a 19th century historian, with an almost perceptible sneer, described the United States as having a "pharisaical self-righteousness, which is one of the most characteristic traits of the political thought of the masses of the American people." He went on to say that the United States is misguided by "half-true and vague

---

[18] Dean Acheson, *Present at the Creation: My Years in the State Department* (New York: W. W. Norton & Company, 1987), 48.

ideas... to the dignity of unimpeachable principles," by which "the ship of state should be steered."[19] He was articulating an opinion shared by many frustrated foreigners today that the United States has an absolutely certain belief in its omnicompetence, an unentitled sense of superiority, and an unchecked rapacious appetite that serves its national interests at all costs. This perception dates back to the Monroe Doctrine. Foreigners developed a belief that the policy was a manifestation of "neither disinterested nor unselfish, but rather an indisputable evidence of [U.S.] overweening national conceit." [20] Antipathy stems from the United States' failure to reign in its hubris.

Why Public Opinion Matters

Since the time when Thomas Jefferson insisted upon a "decent respect to the opinions of mankind," public opinion has controlled foreign policy in all democracies.

Secretary of State Cordell Hull, 1936

Global perception and the reasons for antipathy are important because diplomacy does not occur in a vacuum. Disgruntled or distrustful populations are the driving force behind most domestic politics, which can turn otherwise amenable politicians into difficult international negotiating partners. For example, this could translate into lost

---

[19] Hermann Von Holst, "The Constitutional and Political History of the United States", 8 vols. (1876-1892): I, 34, 74, quoted in Jerald A. Combs, *American Diplomatic History: Two Centuries of Changing Interpretations* (Berkeley: University of California Press, 1985), 47.

[20] Hiram Bigham, "The Monroe Doctrine: An Obsolete Shibboleth", (New Haven, 1913):pages 6-7 quoted in Jerald A. Combs, *American Diplomatic History: Two Centuries of Changing Interpretations* (Berkeley: University of California Press, 1985), 102.

leverage during trade agreement negotiation if politicians feel compelled to kowtow to an uniformed public. Understanding what triggers antipathy allows one to adapt behavior and formulate strategy that appropriately understand the contextual environment. "Publics matter to governments as tools of national foreign policy."[21]

Nicholas Spykman, one of the founders of the classical realist school in U.S. foreign policy, once explained that power in international relations is also, "influenced by love, hate, and charity, by moral indignation and the hope of material gain, by the moods and psychological abnormalities of rulers, and by the emotional afflictions of peoples."[22]

Conclusion

Undeniably, the United States has had, and continues to have, significant influence in world affairs thanks to its economic might. As stated by Secretary of State Hilary Clinton, "a strong economy has been a quiet pillar of American power in the world. It gives [the United States] the leverage needed to exert influence and advance [U.S.] interests. It gives other countries confidence in [U.S.] leadership and a greater stake in partnering with [the U.S.]."[23] She went on to say, "America's economic strength and [its] global leadership are a package deal."[24] The interplay discussed throughout this thesis has demonstrated how military and economic might became the two pillars that

---

[21] Brian Hocking et all, *The New Public Diplomacy: Soft Power in International Relations*, ed. Jan Melissan, (New York, Palgrave Macmillan, 2007), 41.

[22] Jerald A. Combs, *American Diplomatic History: Two Centuries of Changing Interpretations* (Berkeley: University of California Press, 1985), 202.

[23] Leslie H. Gelb, "Hillary Hits the Mark" TheDailyBeast.com, October 14, 2011, http://www.thedailybeast.com/articles/2011/10/14/hillary-clinton-speech-to-economic-club-of-new-york-a-brilliant-moment.html (accessed April 10, 2012)

[24] Josh Rogin, "State Department to Hire New Chief Economist" ForeignPolicy.com, October 14, 2011, under "The Cable," http://thecable.foreignpolicy.com/posts/2011/10/14/state_department_to_hire_new_chief_economist (accessed February 2, 2012)

underpin U.S. hegemony. The document has also explained how the United States uses its diplomatic instrument of power to leverage the influence it garners from being a world leader.

U.S. diplomacy has been reactive to the interplay and has directly and indirectly used U.S. economic and military strength to compel action from foreign nations. Those two pillars are showing signs of becoming less robust. As their strength falters, and as global resentment of unilateral U.S. supremacy grows, an evolution in diplomacy will have to occur in order for U.S. influence to retain its primacy. That evolution starts with diplomacy becoming more proactive. An example discussed in detail in the final chapter of this thesis is the engagement of non-traditional sources of power. Chief among the necessary changes, diplomacy must adapt to include interaction with actors and influential players who do not fit the contemporary mold of diplomatic interlocutors.

CHAPTER 6: RECOMENDATIONS

Expanding Engagement Beyond Nation-states

The U.S. government clearly recognizes the existence and importance of international systems. Multilateral diplomacy is centered on that concept. However, the world's issues are now too complex to all be pigeonholed into archaic frameworks intended for the nation-state model. The U.S. government must not only grasp the importance of transnational (across nations) and supranational (above nations) entities, it must decide to engage them diplomatically. Ideological friction exists external to governments. We no longer live in a world where national threats emanate solely from within countries' ruling political parties and their policies. Religious, tribal, cultural, and global corporations have social bases and are now actors on the stage of world politics. These disaggregated entities have inherent conflicts in their interests and pursuits. That ideological strife at times is directed at other non-nation-state entities, as witnessed for example during tribal clashes. However, that discord can be directed by a supranational actor against a nation-state, as demonstrated by terrorist attacks on the United States. Unless U.S. diplomacy evolves to officially interact with these transnational and supranational players, the United States will continue to hamper its own ability to achieve resolution.

Global issues today require that U.S. diplomacy develop and use more varied techniques and engage a more diversified set of actors. Areas of instability are fertile ground for political and economic reform, and therefore are critical for diplomatic engagement. U.S. diplomats need to "promote peace and stability in troubled regions, not only through negotiation of treaties in capitals, but also where governments lack authority or scarcely exist, through political stability and economic reconstruction in cities, villages, and provinces."[1] In the absence of a typical diplomatic interlocutor, finding a conversant non-conventional entity can result in enormous rewards.

The Department must set aside the accretions of practice and habits of history in order to allow for this shift in organizational culture. By repackaging sentiments already in circulation and announcing a push to expand engagement in the 2010 Quadrennial Diplomacy and Development Review, Secretary of State Clinton lent weight to the findings of a committee co-chaired by a well respected retired Ambassador, Thomas Pickering and Dr. Barry Blechman. The committee was tasked with fathoming what issues the Department would face in 2025. Engagement beyond the typical paradigm was among its recommendations. [2]

The research conducted for this thesis led to a similar hortatory conclusion: Diplomacy must evolve to routinely engage peripheral, supranational, and non-state actors. The State Department needs an acculturation that must occur at the strategic level, led by upper management at State. Ambassadors in the field then have to take that strategy and translate that into a refinement of current practices at the tactical level -- where mid and entry-level diplomats interact with their interlocutors and suss out emerging, credible atypical actors. In order for this change to occur, the Department must give its full-throated support both within the strategic realm in Washington, and at the operational level run by the Ambassador at each mission. There is a definite need for

---

[1] Harry W. Kopp and Charles A. Gillespie, *Career Diplomacy: Life and Work in the U.S. Foreign Service* (Washington, DC.: Georgetown University Press, 2008), page 193.

[2] Advisory Committee on Transformational Diplomacy: Final Report of the State Department in 2025 Working Group, (Washington, DC., 2008), 15.

diplomacy to take an active interest in expanding its focus beyond the political class of

state policy makers and intellectuals in order to connect with emerging sources of

influence. U.S. diplomats need to be actively seeking credible non-conventional sources

of influence.

Economic Statecraft

The Department of State created a new Under Secretary for Economic Affairs in

1946 in response to complexity that foreign aid created. Again the Department is in need

of developing additional economic expertise. In February 2012, Secretary of State

Clinton described a strategy for developing tools of "economic statecraft," which is

designed to expand the Department's involvement in economic engagement programs in

the economic arena.[3] While this new initiative calls for a sub-national dialogue, this

thesis takes that a step further and urges that the dialogue be conducted with

contemporary and non-contemporary actors alike. The best way for diplomacy to

contend with the increased complexity of future trends discussed in Chapter 5 is to

include dialogue with non-traditional actors in its repertoire.

This sort of engagement with unofficial actors has precedence in the already

developed relationships between embassies and U.S. commercial entities. "Connections

between America's official and unofficial presence overseas have been growing in

breadth, depth, and complexity. The unofficial presence -- investors, exporters,

importers, charities, groups that preach, teach, or advocate, and purveyors of the globally

---

[3] Josh Rogin, "State Department to Hire New Chief Economist" ForeignPolicy.com, October 14, 2011, under "The Cable," http://thecable.foreignpolicy.com/posts/2011/10/14/state_department_to_hire_new_chief_economist (accessed February 2, 2012)

pervasive American popular culture -- dwarfs the official presence in almost every way."[4]

There is a vitality that accompanies strenuous engagement with the world, not just contemporary interlocutors. "Relationships between embassies and the private groups operating in their countries are like diplomatic relationships between allies: they aim at maintaining the alignment of interests and working in tandem where possible, and, when interests diverge, at staying in close touch, avoiding open conflict, and finding areas of cooperation that can be expanded over time."[5] This can be extrapolated to an institutional drive to engage non-traditional actors of all sorts.

Smart Diplomacy

"The United States is engaged in regional and global conflicts that are at least as political as they are military. Over 11 percent of our population, more than thirty-one million people, are foreign born. Foreign trade is one-quarter of our economy. Environmental changes, epidemic and pandemic diseases, even financial panics sweep across borders and cannot be controlled unilaterally…Whenever and wherever we can, we need to shape events to our advantage."[6] If unity of effort can benefit NATO's concept of smart defense, so could it benefit what this thesis coins as "smart diplomacy." In these times of fiscal austerity, the United States has found value in pooling and sharing defense resources under the rubric of smart defense. NATO's smart defense concept is

---

[4] Harry W. Kopp and Charles A. Gillespie, *Career Diplomacy: Life and Work in the U.S. Foreign Service* (Washington, DC.: Georgetown University Press, 2008), 194.

[5] Harry W. Kopp and Charles A. Gillespie, *Career Diplomacy: Life and Work in the U.S. Foreign Service* (Washington, DC.: Georgetown University Press, 2008), 194.

[6]. Zbigniew Brzezinski, *The Choice: Global Domination or Global Leadership* (New York: Basic Books, 2004), 16.

about pooling and sharing capabilities, setting priorities and better coordinating efforts. "Smart Diplomacy" would be the pooling and sharing of diplomatic resources with nations with which the United States consistently works in extremely close cooperation, such as the Five Eyes nations. This recommendation advocates a different employment of existing diplomatic corps resources, not an increase in personnel. It is an evolution in how the United States would use its diplomats, not in how many it would hire and deploy.

The main thrust of the concept would be to recognize that some of the Five Eyes nations have deep historic colonial, ethnic or cultural ties to other nations of common interest. Those Five Eyes nations are therefore better attuned to deciphering who potential non-conventional actors could be and what relevance they have. The United States already has a strong bilateral ties with these nations because of common values, interests, and security concerns. By developing a method for pooling diplomatic resources, the Department of State would be able to benefit significantly from the insight those nations could provide.

Connecting With a Domestic Base

The U.S. population has become apathetic towards international affairs. When the public is uninformed and it is only a small circle of conversant power players and intellectual elite who understand the linkages between national interests and foreign affairs, it is the Department of State that struggles to contend with a distorted image of the United States as the benevolent arbiter of good and evil. When there is negative global blowback, the U.S. public does not understand the reasons for it and in response its knee-jerk reaction is to tend towards isolationism and cut foreign aid funding and other useful programs. The absence of a connection with a domestic constituency makes it much harder to advocate for adequate funding to keep diplomacy on a steady course. Secretary of State Dean Acheson once noted that many Americans do not want to hear too much about the complexities of foreign affairs.[7] Generally speaking, the U.S. public is not interested in learning about these complexities, or understanding that the world holds differing viewpoints from which political action occurs. The "believers in American omnipotence, to whom every goal unattained is explicable only by incompetence or treason,"[8] are more fond of blaming the Department of State when the world does not behave in accordance with U.S. desires.

On the opposite end of the spectrum are the Americans who bring deeply held political opinions because of their ties to countries from which they or their families emigrated. "The United States is a nation of immigrants or the descendant of immigrants. Most of the older stock has lost its sentimental ties with the Mother Country, but the newer stock has retained ancient loyalties. When wars, revolutions, and persecutions have convulsed the homeland, Irish-hyphen-Americans, German-hyphen-American, Polish-hyphen-Americans, Jewish-hyphen-Americans, and others have brought pressure on the Washington government to shape foreign policy in their interests. The result has been that the United States has often not been able to speak to the outside world with the authority of one voice."[9]

---

[7] Kopp and Gillespie, *Career Diplomacy: Life and Work in the U.S. Foreign*, page 10.

[8] Acheson, *Present at the Creation: My Years in the State Department*, page 303

[9] Thomas A. Bailey, *Diplomatic History of the American People* (Englewood Cliffs, N.J.,: Prentice-Hall, 1974) page 4

If the majority of Americans remain disinterested and non-participatory, the vocal group, no matter if representing a minority, will dictate policy. In order for diplomacy to act on behalf of the entire nation, the Department of State must find a way to reach out and connect with a domestic base.

However much the U.S. public may flirt with isolationist notions, in reality the United States cannot afford to do so if the current way of life is to be preserved. The United States depends on international trade and cooperation, and is becoming increasingly dependent on collective defense as budgets shrink. The U.S. public must understand its role in global interactions -- political, economic, legal, social, etc. -- and must participate responsibly. If the United States too forcefully grips the fragile reigns of global social order, hegemony will be lost. Equally important to recognize is if the U.S. public fails to understand the necessity to engage, those reigns will fall out of grasp.

The United States needs to raise its level of public debate and deepen the U.S. populace's understanding of how global events and U.S. participation have a direct impact on daily life -- from security from existential threats, to agricultural trade and industry commerce. It all affects their personal and economic well being. The American public understands the purpose of a standing military. Likewise, they need an understanding of the value in having a diplomatic corps. This improved understanding not only will debunk myths of grossly overestimated use of tax revenue for foreign aid, it will also create "buy in" where the population takes ownership.

The U.S. public needs to extricate itself from the catatonic state it is in before memory of civic participation is so atrophied that reviving it is out of the realm of possibility. Sadly, the rhythm of the domestic political cycle encourages populist theatrics that deter the nation from responsibly governing.

In May 2012 a bipartisan amendment that would affect the 1948 law on how the U.S. government manages its public diplomacy was inserted into the latest defense authorization bill. It is intended to update the law to reflect how information is shared via the internet now and "gives Americans the chance to see what the State Department is saying to people all over the world."[10] If passed, this legislation would make it possible for the Department of State to connect with a domestic base.

Strategy Amidst Austerity

When an organization cannot afford to restructure, grow the force, or simply throw money at a problem, it has to examine its overarching strategy. "All foreign service agencies are adjusting the way they use their foreign service members to match changes in the global distribution of economic and political power and the shifting location of strategic threats."[11] Like other U.S. agencies, the Department of State must review its strategy and employment of increasingly limited resources in order to meet critical national interests.

Interagency Cross-fertilization

The concept of interagency cooperation is not new. The Department of Defense sends military aids to staff various positions within the State Department. The

---

[10] Josh Rogin, "Much Ado About State Department 'Propaganda'" ForeignPolicy.com, May 23, 2012, under "The Cable," http://thecable.foreignpolicy.com/posts/2012/05/23/much_ado_about_state_department_propaganda (accessed June 3, 2012)

[11] Kopp and Gillespie, *Career Diplomacy: Life and Work in the U.S. Foreign Service*, 194.

Department of State, albeit on a small scale given the difference in overall size, sends Foreign Policy Advisors (POLADs) on secondment to key Defense headquarters. While these advisors do their part to represent their home services while on loan, the practice is still quite ad hoc. The need is for more institutionalized interagency deliberative long-term planning below the Principals and Deputy Principals level at the National Security Council still exists. As it stands, this level of planning only occurs when a crisis or imminent threat compels it. The Government Accountability Office prepared a report in 2012 that aimed to decide what professional development activities the nine key national security agencies[12] regularly conducted in order to develop a whole-of-government approach to protecting the nation and its interests from diverse threats. The report concluded that, "training, interagency rotations, exercises, and other professional development activities can help to improve participants' abilities to collaborate in an increasingly complex national security arena."[13] The report went on to add that gaps in national security staff knowledge and skills pose a barrier to the interagency collaboration needed to address these threats.

For organizational reasons, the different agencies divide the globe along regional boundaries and these boundaries are not identical. Although there is validity in the argument that having different boundaries helps prevent issues from falling through the cracks along the seams, there is also inherent difficulty involved in coordinating systems and processes across multiple agencies and their multiple geographic commands or hubs.

---

[12] The Department of Defense, the Department of State, the U.S. Agency for International Development, the Department of Homeland Security, the Department of Treasury, the Department of Justice, the Department of Energy, the U.S. Department of Agriculture, and the Department of Commerce.

[13] GAO, National Security: An Overview of Professional Development Activities Intended to Improve Interagency Collaboration, GAO-11-108 (Washington, D.C.: November 2010), 28.

The need for institutionalized whole-of-government cross-fertilization should include a focus on understanding the reasons for those different geographic boundaries and therefore should focus on regional issues. "More [interagency] planning and execution should take place at the regional level."[14] State Department Assistant Secretaries of Regional Bureaus need to better understand military end states and priorities within their regions. Current diplomacy is an overwhelming combination of micro-management from across the varied geographic and functional bureaus at the Department of State. Likewise, the Department of Defense Geographic Combatant Commanders need to be more cognizant of civilian objectives and activities.

Not Just Espousing Utopian Principles

Historiography in the aftermath of World War I exposed doubt over the sincerity of U.S. idealistic intentions via expansionist diplomacy. Historians wrote more openly about the economic desires that likely drove political decisions. "While refuting the harshest charges against America's expansionist diplomacy, especially those of the economic determinists, [historians] did agree that American expansion had enough imperialistic characteristics to make the idealistic rationales offered for it seem slightly ridiculous. Still, they were willing to believe these ideals were sincerely held and contained a germ of truth sufficient to allow American statesmen to rationalize pursuit of economic or strategic interest in idealistic terms."[15]

---

[14] Kopp and Gillespie, *Career Diplomacy: Life and Work in the U.S. Foreign Service*, 191.

[15] Jerald A. Combs, *American Diplomatic History: Two Centuries of Changing Interpretations* (Berkeley: University of California Press, 1985), 181.

President Wilson desired a world made safe for democracy. He had "tempered his diplomatic ideals with a highly pragmatic comprehension of the nature of the modern world and both the promises and the dangers it held."[16] Wilson had "shrewdly calculated the reach as well as the limits of American power. Perhaps most importantly, he had been keenly attentive to what kind of foreign policy, resting on principles of moral legitimacy, the American public would reliably support."[17]

Presidents Roosevelt and Truman carried Wilson's aspirations forward. "They asked only that the world be made safe for democracy, not that the entire world forcibly be made democratic."[18] They understood the danger of unilateral action, even if done for laudable reasons. The worldwide surge of anti-Americanism and the palpable erosion of trust in multinational institutions are manifestations of declining U.S. prestige. "In an age awakening to the global dimensions of pandemics, environmental degradation, the fungibility of employment across national frontiers, massive international migrant and refugee flows, the unprecedented scale of international capital transactions, the contagious volatility of financial markets, the planetary menace of nuclear proliferation, not to mention the threat of terrorism, that erosion threatens to deny the world the very tools it needs most to manage the ever more interdependent global order of the twenty-first century."[19]

The Department of State ought to be careful with its rhetoric regarding universal values if it is going to continue to be selective about pressing values issues with some

---

[16] Andrew J. Bacevich, ed., *The Short American Century: a Postmortem* (Cambridge, Mass.: Harvard University Press, 2012), page 36.

[17] Ibid.

[18] Ibid.

[19] Ibid, 37.

countries, like Cuba, and not with others with whom the United States has strategic interests, like China. Although diplomacy should certainly still attempt to give the unheard a voice, and promote respect for human rights, being dogmatic in its rhetoric will further restrict U.S. potentialities. By making emulation of the United States' utopian model a prerequisite for future providential engagement, the United States lays out restrictive conditions that restrict its ability to make strategic, rather than formulaic, foreign policy decisions without appearing duplicitous and insincere. This recommendation is not about discarding efforts to improve universal values. Rather it is a pragmatic concern for the loss of credibility as a consequence of perceived hypocrisy.

Shaping Global Perceptions

The battle of global perceptions is a struggle for legitimacy and is often won by establishing primacy. Governments create a narrative based on their target audience. Audiences with reputable beliefs are targeted because if successfully swayed, their favorable perception bestows credibility on the government attempting to shape perceptions. If the governmental organization is able to tap into the audience's ideological and sentimental thought process, power in the form of influence is temporarily transferred to the organization.

Nations use various elements of national power to shape perceptions. For example, diplomacy is employed to create a favorable information environment in foreign arenas so that U.S. friendly ideas can be promulgated. This is an example of shaping perceptions through passive human interaction. Diplomats continuously work to build and maintain a perception that is advantageous to U.S. interests. While the need for this may seem obvious after conflict, it occurs before and during as well. In fact, it is during conflict that these narratives must be most carefully used.

U.S. politicians are often short-sighted when it comes to grasping the value in foreign perceptions. They undervalue the power that comes with harnessing those perceptions. The Department of State needs to clearly articulate how valuable this is during strategic level U.S. foreign policy formulation for it is the continuous retuning and refining of diplomacy as global circumstances and perceptions change that will protect the United States' primacy.

CONCLUSION

U.S. economic interests have historically had a hand in driving the creation of new foreign policy, which in turn has driven the creation of new diplomacy. Charles Seymour, a noted historian of U.S. diplomacy, wrote in 1935 that, "if America abandoned its economic weapons for isolation, it would be driven to build an armament of such size as to stand alone against any invasion of America's vital rights."[1] Mr. Seymour was describing a balance between U.S. economic and military might. This document took that description a step further and linked the balance of U.S. economic and military instruments of national power to that of its international standing -- its hegemony -- and illustrated how diplomacy has evolved and been used to improve that balance and further national interests.

As demonstrated in the historical review, each time the United States emerged victorious in various conflicts, diplomacy was elevated in prominence. Often, the Department of State benefited financially from the resultant "peace dividend" and underwent reorganization and grew in size. With that newly intensified prominence, diplomacy set about identifying and achieving increasingly greater economic influence that would benefit U.S prosperity. Over the course of the first four chapters this thesis limned the interrelationship between the three dynamics, beginning with the Spanish-American War, and ending with the aftermath of World War II.

---

[1] Charles Seymour, "American Neutrality, 1914 - 1917," (New Haven and London, 1935): pages 175 - 180, quoted in Jerald A. Combs, *American Diplomatic History: Two Centuries of Changing Interpretations* (Berkeley: University of California Press, 1985), 150.

Military strength is a manifestation of economic ability. How that economic ability is projected internationally influences international perceptions, which then largely shape how effective diplomacy is. The interrelationship grew incrementally in strength between the late 1800s and the early 21st century. The synergistic interplay of these three elements of national power, and their strategic use, provided the United States with a peerless level of dominance and allowed for great flexibility in how the United States conducted diplomacy. However, since roughly 2009 conditions have changed significantly enough to have forced an imbalance in that tripartite relationship. U.S. hegemony has weakened as global antipathy has grown, while the United States has suffered a decline in its economic and military strengths. This paper has argued that an evolution in diplomacy will have to occur in order for U.S. influence to retain its primacy. That evolution starts with diplomacy becoming more proactive and less reactive. Chief among the necessary changes, diplomacy must adapt to include interaction with actors and influential players who do not fit the contemporary mold of diplomatic interlocutors.

BIBLIOGRAPHY

Acheson, Dean. *Present at the Creation: My Years in the State Department*. New York: W. W. Norton & Company, 1987.

Advisory Committee on Transformational Diplomacy. *Final Report of the State Department in 2025 Working Group* (Washington D.C.: 2008).

Bacevich, Andrew J., ed. *The Short American Century: a Postmortem*. Cambridge, Mass.: Harvard University Press, 2012.

Bailey, Thomas A. *A Diplomatic History of the American People*. 9th ed. 2 vols. Englewood Cliffs, N.J.,: Prentice-Hall, 1974.

Black, Conrad. *Richard M. Nixon: a Life in Full*. New York: Public Affairs, 2007.

Blechman, Dr. Barry; Pickering, Thomas; and Gingrich, Newt. *Advisory Committee on Transformational Diplomacy: Final Report of the State Department in 2025 Working Group*, (Washington, DC., 2008).

Brzezinski, Zbigniew. *The Choice: Global Domination or Global Leadership*. New York: Basic Books, 2004.

Chadwick, French Ensor. *The Relations Of The United States And Spain: Diplomacy*. Kessinger Publishing, LLC, 2007.

Chow, Eugene and Weitz, Richard. *Rebuilding Diplomacy: A Survey of Past Calls for State Department Transformation* (Washington D.C.:August 2010).

Combs, Jerald A. *American Diplomatic History: Two Centuries of Changing Interpretations*. Berkeley: University of California Press, 1985.

Dorman, Andrew, and Greg Kennedy, eds. *War and Diplomacy: from World War I to the War On Terrorism*. Washington, D.C.: Potomac Books Inc., 2008.

Dorman, Shawn, ed. *Inside a U.S. Embassy: Diplomacy at Work*. 3rd ed. Washington, D.C.: Potomac Books Inc., 2011.

Frederick, Olivia Mae. *Henry P. Fletcher and United States-Latin American Policy, 1910-1930 (Dissertations in American Biography)*. Arno Press, 1982.

Fuller, J.F.C. *The Conduct of War, 1789-1961: a Study of the Impact of the French, Industrial, and Russian Revolutions On War and Its Conduct*. New York: Da Capo Press, 1992.

GAO, *National Security: An Overview of Professional Development Activities Intended to Improve Interagency Collaboration*, GAO-11-108 (Washington, D.C.: November 2010).

Gelb, Leslie H. "Hillary Hits the Mark" TheDailyBeast.com, October 14, 2011, http://www.thedailybeast.com/articles/2011/10/14/hillary-clinton-speech-to-economic-club-of-new-york-a-brilliant-moment.html (accessed April 10, 2012)

Hockin, Brian, *The New Public Diplomacy: Soft Power in International Relations*, ed. Jan Melissan. New York, Palgrave Macmillan, 2007.

Immerman, Richard H. "Eisenhower and Dulles: Who Made the Decisions?" *Political Psychology* Vol. 1, No. 2 (August 1979).

Kissinger, Henry. *White House Years.* New York: Simon & Schuster, 2011.

Kopp, Harry W. and Charles A. Gillespie. *Career Diplomacy: Life and Work in the U.S. Foreign Service.* Washington, DC.: Georgetown University Press, 2008.

Lansford, Tom. *Theodore Roosevelt in Perspective.* New York: Nova Science Pub Inc, 2005.

Mahbubani, Kishore. *Can Asians Think?* 3rd ed. Singapore: Times Editions, 2004.

Moran, Theodore H. *American Economic Policy and National Security.* New York: Council on Foreign Relations, 1993.

Paterson, Thomas, J. Garry Clifford, Shane J. Maddock, Deborah Kisatsky, and Kenneth Hagan. *American Foreign Relations: a History.* 7th ed. Boston, MA.: Wadsworth Publishing, 2009.

Roark, James L., Michael P. Johnson, Patricia Cline Cohen, Sarah Stage, and Susan M. Hartmann. *The American Promise: a History of the United States.* 4th ed. Boston, MA.: Bedford/St. Martin's, 2009.

Rogin, Josh. "State Department to Hire New Chief Economist." ForeignPolicy.com. October 14, 2011, under "The Cable," http://thecable.foreignpolicy.com/posts/2011/10/14/state_department_to_hire_new_chief_economist (accessed February 2, 2012)

Rogin, Josh. "Much ado about State Department 'Propaganda'" ForeignPolicy.com. May 23, 2012, under "The Cable," http://thecable.foreignpolicy.com/posts/2012/05/23/much_ado_about_state_department_propaganda (accessed June 3, 2012)

United States Office of the Director of National Intelligence, ed. *Global Trends 2025: A Transformed World*. 4, Unclassified Report ed. Washington, DC: Central Intelligence Agency, 2008.

United States Department of State Office of the Historian, "A Short History of the Department of State," http://history.state.gov/departmenthistory/short-history (accessed January 23, 2012).

United States Department of State Office of the Historian, "Milestones: 1914 - 1920, American Entry into World War I, 1917" http://history.state.gov/milestones/1914-1920/WWI (accessed February 5, 2012).

Weaver, Frederick S. *The United States and the Global Economy: from Bretton Woods to the Current Crisis*. Lanham: Rowman & Littlefield Publishers, 2011.

William Howard Taft: "Fourth Annual Message," December 3, 1912. Online by Gerhard Peters and John T. Woolley, The American Presidency Project. http://www.presidency.ucsb.edu/ws/?pid=29553 (accessed February 18, 2012).

Zakaria, Fareed. *From Wealth to Power: The Unusual Origins of America's World Role*. Princeton: Princeton University Press, 1999.